KidKit

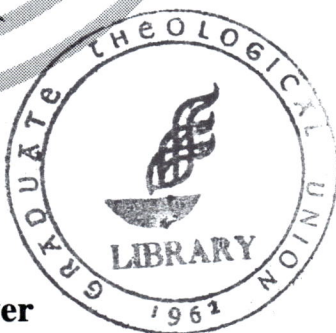

Bonnie J. Hinkemeyer
Illustrations by Daniel Jankowski

CSS Publishing Company, Inc., Lima, Ohio

KID KIT

Library of Congress Cataloging-in-Publication Data

Hinkemeyer, Bonnie J., 1959-
  Kidkit : entertaining ideas and activities for children /
Bonnie J. Hinkemeyer.
     p.   cm.
  ISBN 0-7880-0727-0 (pbk.)
  1. Creative activities and seatwork. 2. Amusements. I.
Title.
LB1027.25.H55   1997
371.3'97—dc20   96-38673
CIP

ISBN: 0-7880-0727-0   PRINTED IN U.S.A.

Dedication

To my loving and encouraging father
Harley R. McStott

and to my son
Cole
who inspired this book

TABLE OF CONTENTS

A FEW TIPS TO ENCOURAGE YOUR CHILD'S CREATIVE DEVELOPMENT

• AVOID making art models for children that are too complex. They may become frustrated when they cannot copy what you do.

• GIVE children large sheets of paper so that they can use large arm movements. Later, when they develop more control and have developed good hand movements, smaller sheets can be used.

• MAKE a variety of art materials available to your child — paints, play dough, crayons, and collage materials.

• HAVE a special place where your children can use art materials without having to worry about being too careful. It is also helpful if this area is easy to clean up after projects.

• TRY not to ask what children are making, because this may make them feel pressured to produce art work that stands up to adult standards. Children do a lot of experimenting with materials, textures, and colors which need not represent anything. It takes a long time for some to be able to produce symbolic or representational art work.

• COMMENT on the process of the art activity. In other words, it is fine to say, "That certainly is an interesting color you made when you mixed purple and yellow," but, again, if you really want to know about a picture, try saying, "Tell me about your picture," instead of "Is that a cat?"

• ABOVE all, resist the temptation to redo or change what your children have done. Show them the correct way to hold a scissors or how to apply paste, but let them create on their own. If you want to join in, get a piece of paper and work alongside your children. Have fun and enjoy yourself and your children.

• IT is very important to keep your children's safety uppermost in your mind. Always supervise all the activities in this kit.

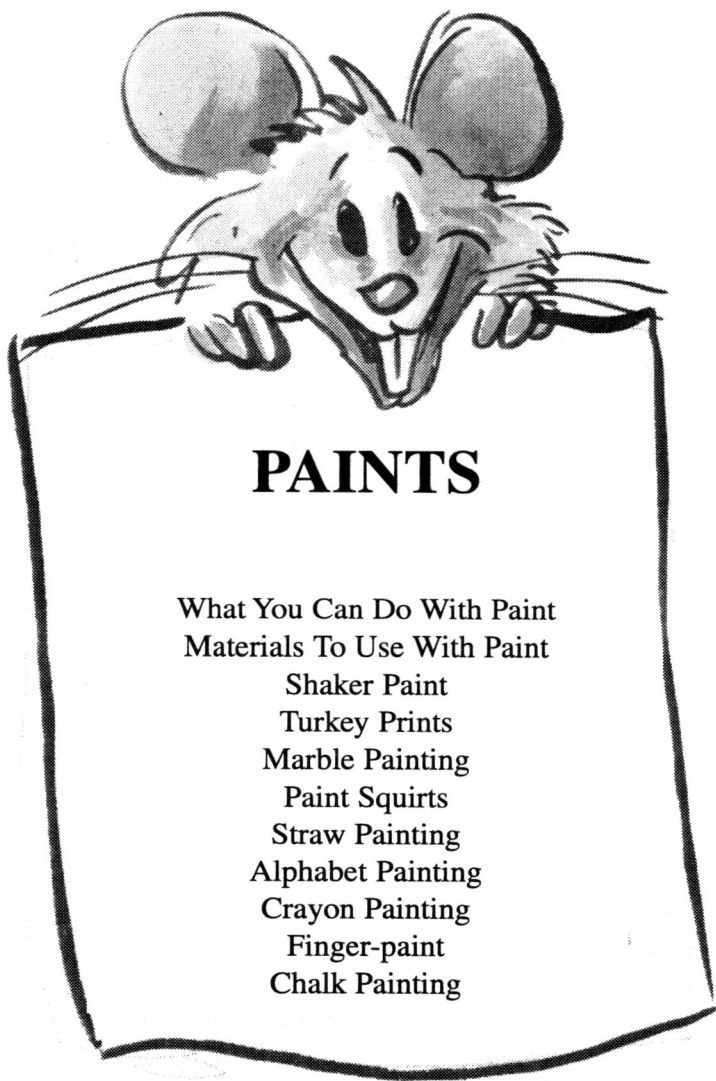

PAINTS

WHAT YOU CAN DO WITH PAINT

Brush, dip, swizzle or spatter it.
Draw in paint with a stick.
Make lines or paint with a fork.
Rake it with a comb.
Paint with toothbrush or Q-tip.
Blow it with a straw.
Print with sponge on the end of a clothespin.
Make handprints or footprints, thumbprints or fingerprints.
Print with corks, pieces of styrofoam, or wood spools.
Print with jar covers, cookie cutters or any kitchen
   implement.

MATERIALS TO USE WITH PAINT

Paint on:
newspaper
fabric
scraps of wood
computer paper
doilies
paper plates
napkins
paper towels
paper bags
paper cups
muffin cups

Paint:
rocks
leaves
pinecones
sea shells
branches
acorns

SHAKER PAINT

Materials: dry tempera paint, moistened construction paper.

Put dry tempera paint in a salt or pepper shaker. Shake the paint over moistened paper. Let dry. You have a unique piece of art.

There is a little magic going on here as the dry paint moistens and takes on brilliant colors. Children will be fascinated by it.

TURKEY PRINTS

Paint your child's fingers and palms. Thumbs should be red, palms brown, and other fingers an assortment of colors to suggest feathers. On individual pieces of paper or on a large piece of paper, have your child spread his/her fingers and make prints of his/her painted hand. Add a couple of legs to each print to complete the turkey.

MARBLE PAINTING

Cut a piece of paper to fit inside a pie tin. Squirt a few drops of liquid paint onto the paper, and place one or two marbles in the tin.

The marbles make a design as they roll through the paint.

Children like the "sound" of painting in this way too!

PAINT SQUIRTS

1/2 cup salt
1/4 cup sugar
2 cups flour
food coloring (optional)

Mix ingredients together and then add water to get a consistency of light cream. Place into any type of squeeze bottle. Excellent pool fun.

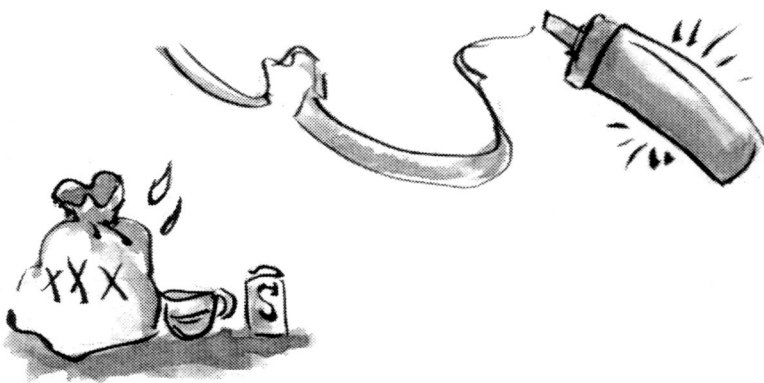

STRAW PAINTING

In a location where some spattered paint can be controlled or contained, pour small pools of colored paint on paper. With a regular drinking straw, have the child blow at the pools of paint in various directions. Gentle blowing is best. The result is a free mixing of colors in abstract forms and sunbursts which can be very dramatic and exciting.

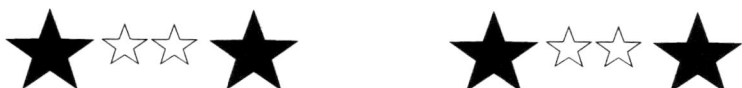

★ ☆☆ ★   ★ ☆☆ ★

ALPHABET PAINTING

Plastic alphabet letters and numbers can be dipped into paint and then pressed onto paper. Your child will enjoy the printing of letters. Through this process comes an understanding of and recognition of basic letter and number shapes. Some simple words can be made — the child's name, DOG, CAT, etc. When the child can count, objects can be counted and the number printed on the page.

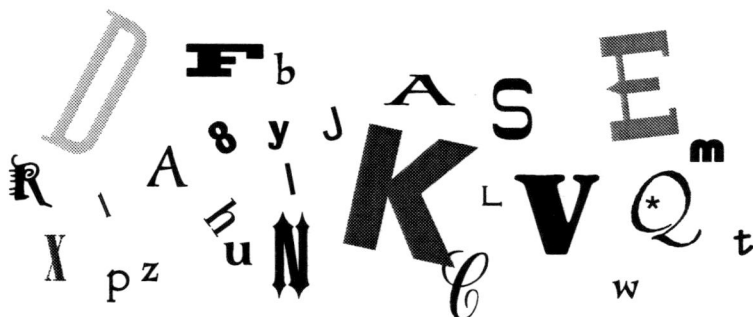

CRAYON PAINTING

Materials: towel, crayons, finger-paint paper.

Fold a towel in half and place it on the table. Fold finger-paint paper in half and place on top of towel. Peel old crayons and shave bits of crayon onto one side of paper with vegetable peeler. Pre-shave crayons for very young children. Fold blank side of paper over crayon side. Press gently with iron set at lowest temperature, no steam. Open paper slowly. Crayons will look like paints.

FINGER-PAINT

Materials: newspaper, tape, sponge, liquid starch,
    powdered tempera, fingerprint paper.

Cover table with newspaper and tape in place. Place fingerprint paper in center of newspaper. Wet sponge and wring out extra water. Wipe sponge across paper to dampen it. Pour a couple of tablespoons of liquid starch onto the paper. Sprinkle powdered tempera directly onto starch. Mix with the palm of the hand.

Make swirls with the palms, rounds with the fists, and lines with fingers. Add a few sprinkles of another color and mix in.

CHALK PAINTING

Materials: liquid starch, colored chalk, aerosol hair spray.

Pour a small amount of liquid starch into a bowl. Place colored chalk in the starch. Let soak a minute. Draw a picture on paper with the wet chalk. Let the picture dry completely before moving. To preserve chalk pictures, spray them with aerosol hair spray outdoors or in a well-ventilated room.

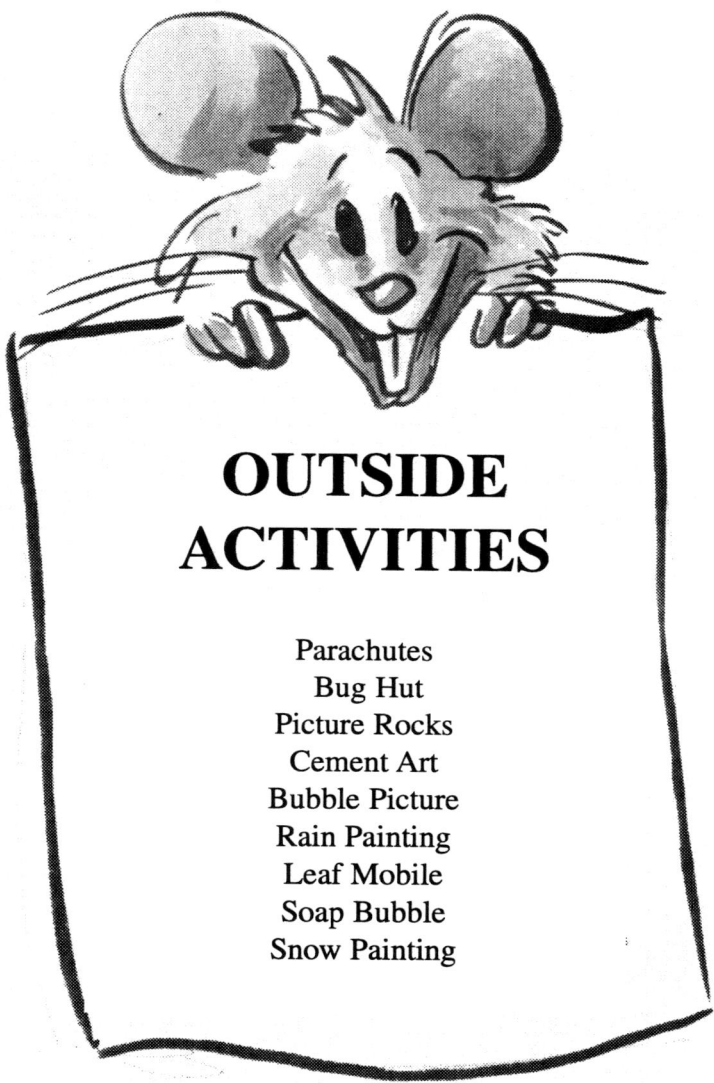

OUTSIDE
ACTIVITIES

Parachutes
Bug Hut
Picture Rocks
Cement Art
Bubble Picture
Rain Painting
Leaf Mobile
Soap Bubble
Snow Painting

PARACHUTES

To make a parachute, tie 12-inch strings to the corners of napkins or fabric squares, gather the strings at the bottom, and tie them to a weighted object. Toss the parachute into the air and watch it slowly descend.

BUG HUT

Cut out two sides of a half-gallon milk carton and put the carton inside a nylon stocking. Tie a knot in the stocking.

This hut makes a nice home for caterpillars, beetles, and grasshoppers. Lunch for them includes leaves, grass, bits of bread, and always a capful of water. The bugs should be released in one or two days.

PICTURE ROCKS

Mix some powdered tempera paint into sand or salt to color it.

Have the children draw a picture or shape on a rock with liquid glue. Next, have them sprinkle the shape or picture with the colored sand or salt. Shake off the excess and allow to dry.

CEMENT ART

If there is a cement sidewalk or cement slab nearby, an entertaining outside activity is to let the children draw designs, pictures, and shapes on the cement with colored chalk. This project cleans up easily with a garden hose. The children can help clean up the cement with sponges or rags.

BUBBLE PICTURE

Make a bubble mixture by mixing 1 tbsp. liquid dish detergent, 4 tbsp. water, and 1 tbsp. food coloring.

Have the children place a straw in the cup of bubble mixture and blow up a mound of bubbles.

Lay a piece of paper over the bubbles. As the bubbles touch the paper, they form a beautiful design.

RAIN PAINTING

Give each child a paper plate and let them sprinkle a few drops of food coloring onto it. Have them dress in protective clothing, then walk outside to hold their plates in the rain for about a minute. Encourage them to notice the unique designs created by the rain. Allow the plates to dry.

LEAF MOBILE

Use either pressed or fresh autumn leaves. Spread the leaves out on paper. Cut pieces of thread in different lengths. Apply a thin coat of glue to the surface of each leaf. Cover the entire leaf. Put an end of a piece of thread at the top of each leaf and fasten it there with the glue. Let dry.

On their threads of different lengths, you can fasten the leaves to a light fixture or hang them from a coat hanger to make a colorful mobile.

SOAP BUBBLE

Fill the bottom of a cake pan with about 1/2 inch of water. Add four squirts of a liquid dishwashing detergent. Mix the solution gently. A plastic soda six-pack holder is excellent for making lots of bubbles. Dip the plastic holder into the soapy water and wave it through the air.

SNOW PAINTING

Pre-mix powdered tempera paint to a creamy consistency. Have your child paint on the snow or put the tempera into squeeze bottles so the paint can be squeezed onto the snow.

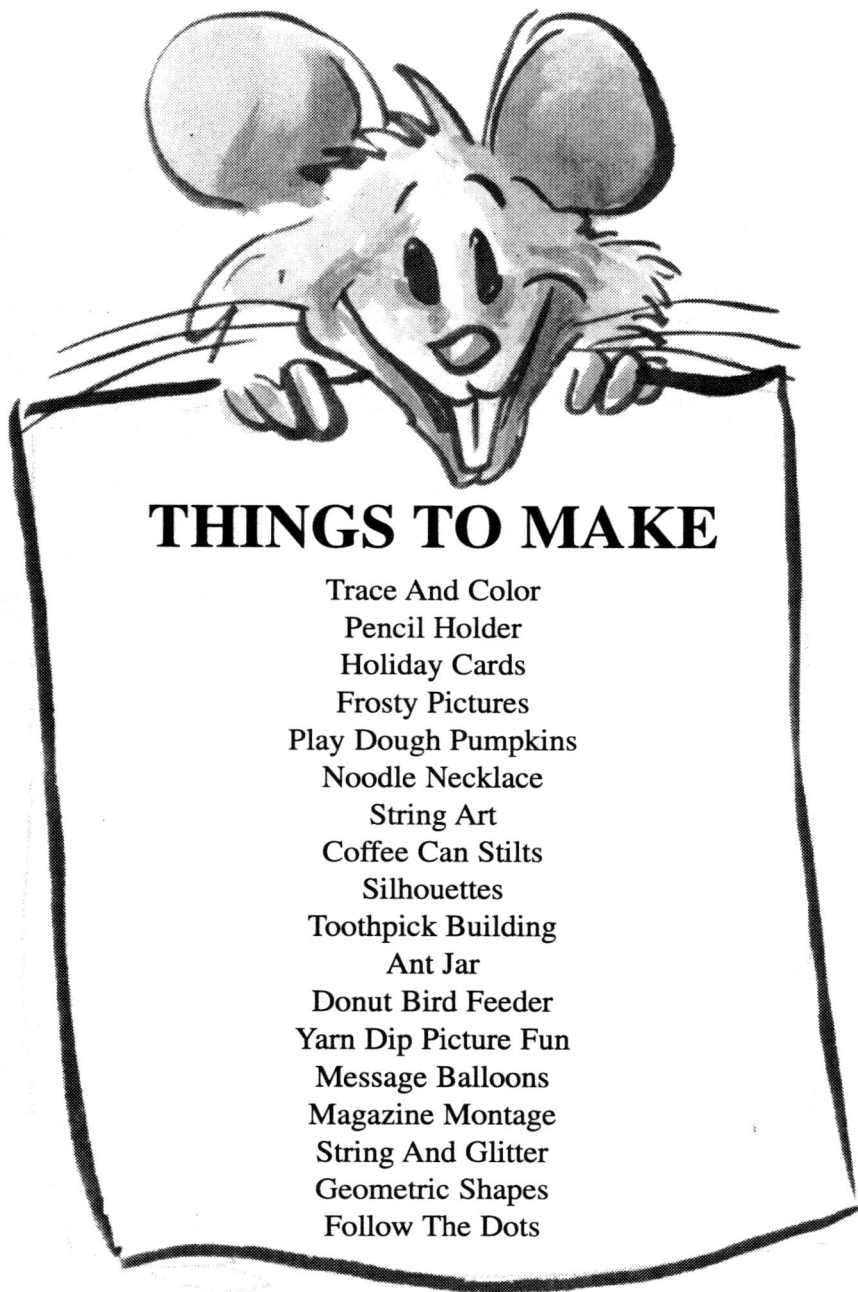

THINGS TO MAKE

Trace And Color
Pencil Holder
Holiday Cards
Frosty Pictures
Play Dough Pumpkins
Noodle Necklace
String Art
Coffee Can Stilts
Silhouettes
Toothpick Building
Ant Jar
Donut Bird Feeder
Yarn Dip Picture Fun
Message Balloons
Magazine Montage
String And Glitter
Geometric Shapes
Follow The Dots

TRACE AND COLOR

You will need a box of animal crackers. The children can trace around the animal crackers with pen or pencil, then the animals can be colored or painted.

PENCIL HOLDER

Have the children tear off small strips of masking tape and put them on the outside of a can, jar or vase, completely covering it. When they finish taping their jars, have them rub on any color of shoe polish.

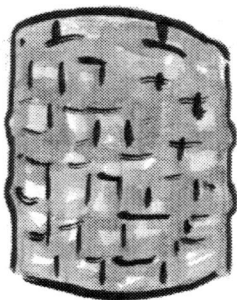

HOLIDAY CARDS

Invite the children each to select a raised design holiday card. Have them lay a plain piece of paper over the raised picture and rub a crayon sideways over the paper. The design of the raised section will appear like magic on the paper.

FROSTY PICTURES

Mix one part Epsom salts to one part boiling water. Let the solution cool.

Have your children draw outdoor pictures or designs on a piece of colored construction paper (snowmen, snowflakes, lakes, rivers, etc.). When they have finished, have them paint their pictures with the cooled Epsom salts solution. As it dries, shiny crystals will form on the picture.

PLAY DOUGH PUMPKINS

Have your children press orange play dough into a plastic lid. Next have them press in some popcorn seeds to make a jack-o-lantern face. Allow the play dough to dry. Then the play dough can be left in the lid or taken out.

NOODLE NECKLACE

Put a teaspoon of food coloring into a cup of warm water. Stir until mixed. If you want brighter colors, add 1/4 teaspoon at a time, until you get the desired color. Cut pieces of string each about two feet long, one for each color you are using. Loop the string around a bobby pin and pass the string through several noodles. Dip them in one of the colors. Soak them for a few minutes, but don't let them get sticky. Spread on a newspaper to dry. Take another length of string about 24-inches long. Loop it around the bobby pin, and string the colored noodles onto it. Mix the colors and shapes as you like. Tie a double knot with the two ends of the string.

STRING ART

In a small bowl put glue, liquid starch, or a flour-and-water paste. Put about 10 feet of fine string or yarn into the bowl. Blow up a balloon. Wipe off excess glue (or starch or paste) from the string and wrap it around and around the balloon. Set aside on wax paper to dry. When fully dry, pop the balloon, creating an open string design.

Options: food coloring can be added to the glue, starch, or paste.

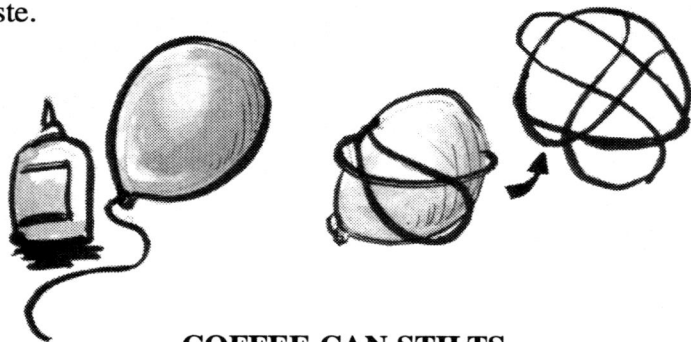

COFFEE CAN STILTS

Some good stilts for beginners can be made from two two-pound coffee cans. (Vegetable cans can be used for smaller children.) Punch two holes, on opposite sides, near the bottom the cans. Thread twine, heavy string or fine rope through the holes for the handles. Two lengths of twine are needed, one for each stilt. With the child standing with one foot on each can, bring the ends of the twine up to his/her hands and tie the ends together. To walk on the stilts, the can is lifted up as a step is taken.

27

SILHOUETTES

A silhouette is actually a paper shadow. To make a child's silhouette, you will need to produce his shadow with a strong light. A large flashlight at a distance of ten feet gives a good, clear shadow. Have the child sit close to a wall, facing right or left. Tape a piece of white drawing paper on the wall behind his/her head. Draw around the outline, then cut out and mount on sturdy paper.

TOOTHPICK BUILDING

You'll need a box of toothpicks and some play dough. Roll the play dough into balls about the size of a pea. Use these as connectors. Stick the toothpicks into the play dough. Building can be as simple or complex as the child's imagina-tion and skill. Put the building aside to dry. In about one day, the joints will harden.

ANT JAR

You'll need 2 clean glass jars, one slightly smaller than the other.

Put the smaller jar without its lid upside down in the center of the larger jar. Fill the space between the jars with loose or sandy soil. Don't pack the soil. To make an ant trap, mix a little bit of sugar with a little water in a small can and lay the can down on its side on the ground near an anthill. Collect about twenty-one ants. The ants must be from the same colony. Put the ants into the ant jar and put the cover on.

The ants will get enough air when you remove the lid for feedings. Once a week only, feed the ants a few grains of grass or bird seed and give them a few drops of sugar water.

DONUT BIRD FEEDER

Find two jar lids about as big around as a donut. Either metal or plastic lids will do. Find a headed nail about 3 inches long. Make a hole in the center of each lid by hammering the nail through, wiggling it around, and pulling it out. Put the nail through one lid, then through the donut hole, then through the other lid. With pliers, bend the pointed end of the nail sideways to keep it from pulling through the lid. Tie a piece of string around the head of the nail and hang outdoors.

Have a bird book handy to answer questions about the birds who come to visit and nibble from this treat.

YARN DIP PICTURE FUN

Use glue or liquid starch or flour-and-water paste to which food coloring can be added. Dip yarn into the glue, starch, or paste and wipe off any excess material. Place yarn on paper or cardboard.

MESSAGE BALLOONS

Lay a balloon flat on a hard surface. With a magic marker, draw designs and messages on the balloon, such as "Happy Birthday" or "Get Well Soon." Allow to dry before inflating.

This is a great way for a child to take part in wishing others well at "his own speed" and with something that he/she enjoys — balloons!

MAGAZINE MONTAGE

Look in old magazines for pictures in variations on a theme. Examples: faces, babies, fruit, vegetables, etc.

Tear out pages, then cut out the pictures. Paste one kind of pictures on manila paper to make a Magazine Montage. Ask children how the pictures are alike and how they are different.

STRING AND GLITTER

Cut string into short, medium, and long pieces. Pour glue into a cup. Dip one string at a time into the glue, stirring with a plastic fork to wet it well.

Lift the string slowly from the cup, pulling it through the fork to prevent tangles.

Lay the wet string in a design on a piece of tin foil. Squiggles or geometric shapes work well.

Sprinkle the wet string with glitter and let dry until hard. Peel the designs off the aluminum foil carefully. Trim unglued ends with scissors and hang them on a bare branch, a Christmas tree, or make a mobile of them.

GEOMETRIC SHAPES

Cut squares, triangles, and circles of different sizes. Cut different kinds of triangles.

Paste shapes onto construction paper to make pictures or random designs.

Try single shape pictures, such as circles on a huge circle or squares on a huge square.

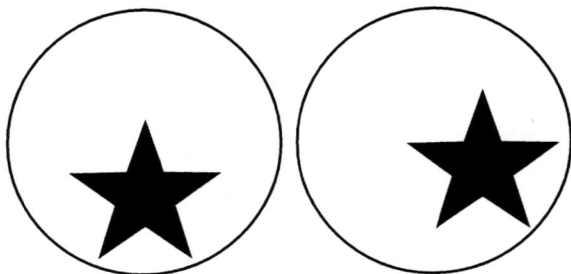

FOLLOW THE DOTS

Draw all sorts of dots on paper at random — along the edges of the paper, in the middle, in bunches, or alone.

Follow the dots with crayons or markers. Dots may be followed more than once and go different ways.

If desired, connect dots with glue, then add yarn.

DISCOVERY AND LEARNING

Thumb Painting
Watch It Rain
Liquid Painting
Snowman
Waterscope
Pencil Holder
Greeting Cards With Leaves
Leaf Drawings
Paper Chains
Button Pictures
Soap Crayons
Drinking Straw Horn
Pot Match
Life-Size Self
Indian Corn
Cut And Cartoon
Water Jar And Toothpicks
Dish Growing
Fizzle Fun Experiment

THUMB PAINTING

Materials: water-based paint, paper, magic markers.

Using water-based paint, have the children dip their thumbs in the paint and press them onto the paper. Using a marker, turn each colored thumbprint into an animal, such as a penguin, mouse, elephant, or kangaroo. Add on eyes, legs, and arms as needed.

WATCH IT RAIN

Show how clouds form in the sky by making a little cloud in a jar. Put about one inch of hot water in a large jar and put a metal pan of ice cubes on top. Then carefully place the jar in a dark place and use a flashlight to look for the cloud. Keep watching to see the tiny raindrops gather and fall to the bottom.

LIQUID PAINTING

Materials: empty roll-on deodorant bottle, white liquid paint.

Fill the bottle with paint. Let your children use the roll-on bottle as a marker to draw designs or pictures on regular paper. Fill more bottles with other colors.

SNOWMAN

Give your child a large piece of construction paper on which to make a large snowman by gluing together many cotton balls. Provide scraps of differently colored construction paper from which the child can cut out facial features, a hat, a pipe and a broom, etc. Paste them on the top of the cotton balls.

WATERSCOPE

Cut the top and bottom off of a milk carton. Using a piece of plastic or a plastic bag, cover one end of the carton. Be sure the plastic is smooth and even around the sides. Put rubber bands over the plastic to hold it in place. You can go to a pond or lake and put the plastic end of the carton into the water. Look into the other end. You'll be able to see fish, rocks, plants, and so forth. This waterscope can also be used in the bathtub.

PENCIL HOLDER

Paint a frozen orange juice or similar can a pretty color. Make a design on one side, painting it on with glue, and then stick on seeds. Or, stripe the can with glue and stick on colored seeds.

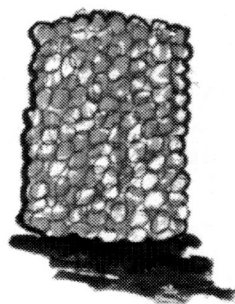

GREETING CARDS WITH LEAVES

Pin a leaf flat on a piece of colored construction paper. Then, using spray paint, spray over the leaf or stipple it with a brush and paint.

If done with holly or a tip of evergreen, this can make an attractive Christmas card.

LEAF DRAWINGS

Collect different leaves from different trees. Place a leaf, soft side down, under a sheet of regular typing paper. With a crayon on its side, your child can color over the leaf. Try another leaf. This makes a beautiful picture. The leaves can then be placed in a magazine and dried. Afterwards, the leaves can be glued to construction paper.

PAPER CHAINS

Cut strips of construction paper or metallic paper about 3/4 inches wide by 6 1/2 inches long.

Before joining them in interlocking circles, print the names of some of your child's friends and family members on the strips. Join the strips with tape or glue.

BUTTON PICTURES

To support the weight of the buttons, use a cardboard background. Provide a variety of buttons for the child to use. After the child has arranged the design, the buttons can be glued to the background.

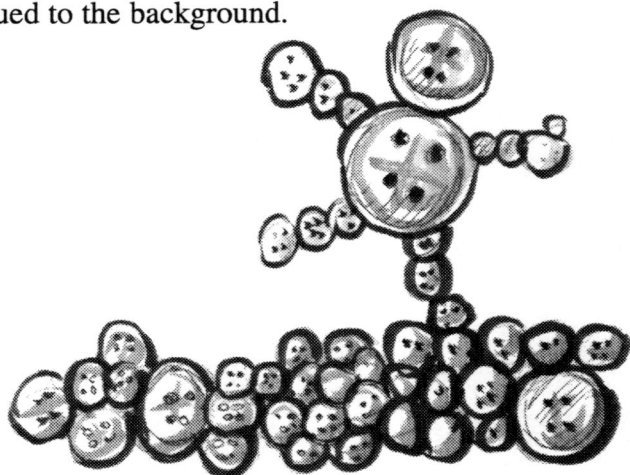

SOAP CRAYONS

Using a one-cup measuring cup, add 1/8 cup water to the cup. Fill the rest of the measuring cup with Ivory Flakes (or grate a bar of Ivory soap). Mix the water and soap flakes together until they form a paste. Add 35 drops of food coloring to the mixture and stir well. Scoop the colored soap mixture out and put it into an ice cube tray, pressing the soap paste down into the cubes until filled to the top. Find a warm place to set the tray for one or two days until firm. Pop out the soap crayons, and they are ready to use.

DRINKING STRAW HORN

Flatten about 1 inch of the end of a drinking straw and crease the sides well. With a scissors, trim the flattened end to a "V." These become the horn reeds. Let the child blow hard into the reed end of the straw. Does the horn work? Sometimes it is necessary to experiment with the length of the reeds — lengthening or shortening them — and with how the child holds them in his/her mouth.

POT MATCH

Kitchen pots and pans can provide a fun game. Put out all your pots and remove the covers. Have your child match the right covers to each pan.

LIFE-SIZE SELF

Roll out a length of brown paper on the floor and have the child lie on it. Trace around the child with a crayon.

Cut out the shape.

Add features and clothes to the Life-Size Self with markers or paint.

INDIAN CORN

Sort Indian corn by color into the cups of a muffin tin. Squirt glue design onto a meat tray. Adjust the top of the glue so that it does not flow too fast. Drop colored corn kernels on top of the glue. Let dry completely.

CUT AND CARTOON

Let the child cut large shapes from ads (oranges, bananas, tires, and so forth). Pre-cut shapes for very young children. Paste the shapes onto paper. Use a black marker to turn the shapes into other things. Example: turn an orange into a fat face, a banana into a boat, a tire into a bike. Experiment with two, three, or more shapes pasted on paper.

WATER JAR AND TOOTHPICKS

Materials: toothpicks, garlic, onion, sweet potato, beet, and potato.

Stick four or five toothpicks in the middle of the vegetable to suspend it in the middle of a glass jar. Fill the jar with water so that the bottom part of the vegetable is submerged.

Check the water every few days and keep the jar filled to the same level. Keep the jar in a sunny location.

In about two weeks a vine or shoot will start to grow.

DISH GROWING

Things you can grow: carrot tops, pineapple tops, turnip tops.

Take about a one-inch slice off the top of the fruit or vegetable and place it in a shallow dish or bowl of water. Keep it in a sunny location, but don't let the water dry out.

New shoots should be visible in about one week.

42

FIZZLE FUN EXPERIMENT

Materials: vinegar, pop bottle, baking soda, and balloons.

Put about 1 inch of vinegar in a pop bottle, then add 2 teaspoons of baking soda to the vinegar. Quickly slip a balloon over the top of the bottle. The balloon is inflated.

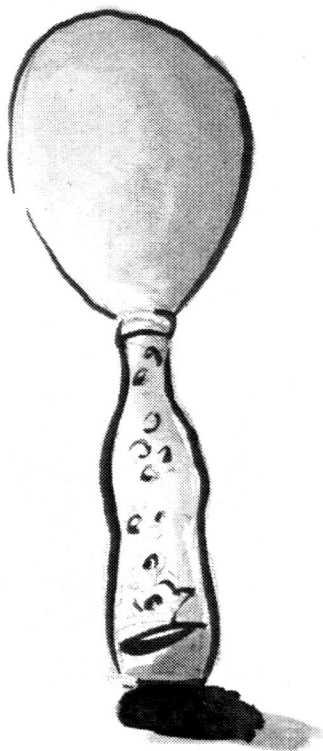

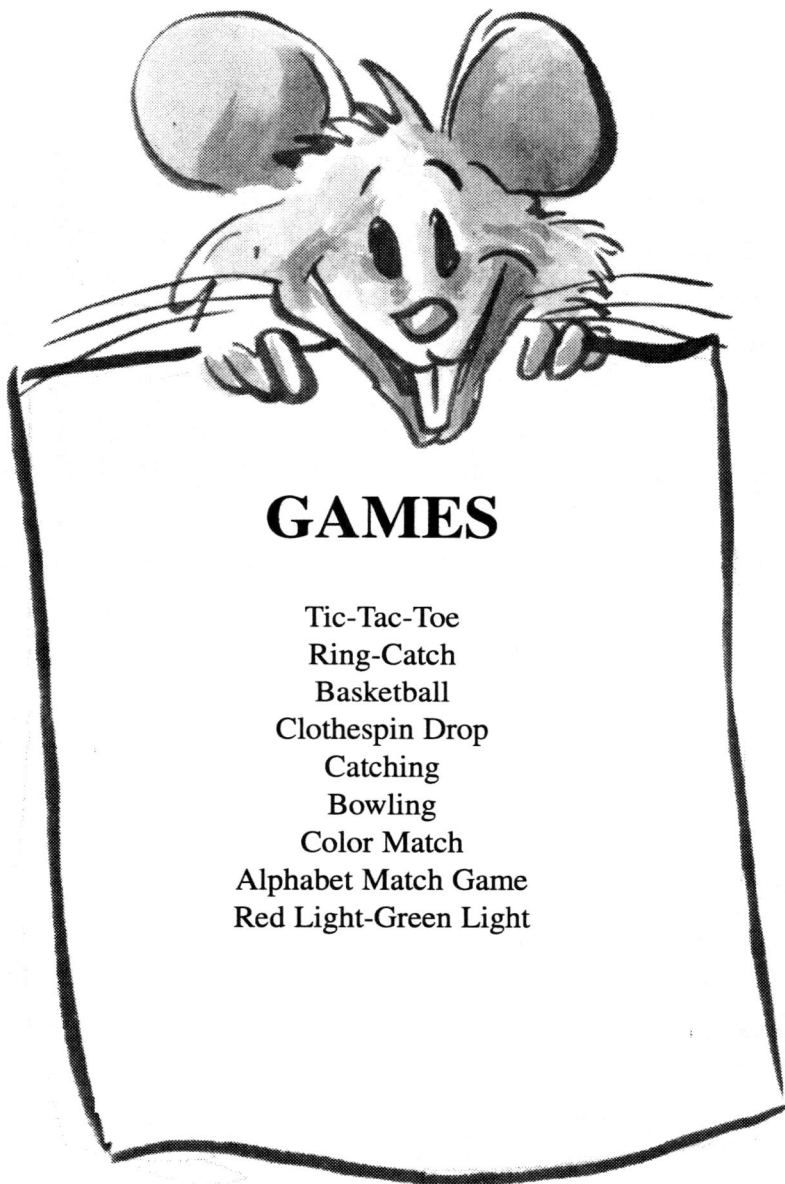

GAMES

Tic-Tac-Toe
Ring-Catch
Basketball
Clothespin Drop
Catching
Bowling
Color Match
Alphabet Match Game
Red Light-Green Light

TIC-TAC-TOE

Draw X's on five milk bottle tops and O's on five more milk bottle tops (or use circles of paper). Draw tic-tac-toe lines on a piece of paper. Now your children have a tic-tac-toe game just their size.

RING-CATCH

Cut out the inside of a plastic lid to make a ring. Punch a hole at one end of a cardboard tube (paper towel tube). Tie the plastic ring onto the tube with a 12-inch length of string. Swing the ring slowly and catch it on the tube.

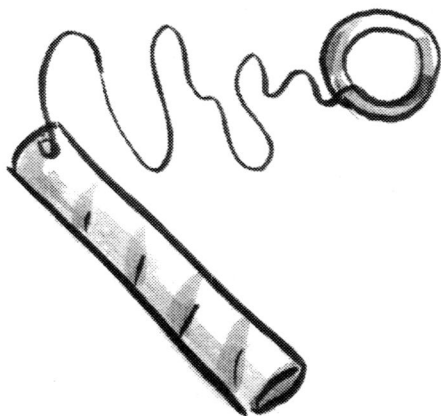

BASKETBALL

Cut the bottom out of an ice cream bucket to make a basketball hoop. Nail the bucket to a post or a tree. Use it like a basketball hoop with a ball or a knotted sock.

CLOTHESPIN DROP

Cut a hole in the top of a plastic milk jug, but leave the handle on. Have the child stand over the jug with straight legs. Drop clothespins into the jug, keeping the hand at chest level while dropping.

CATCHING

Using a styrofoam cup, punch a hole close to the rim of the cup. Tie one end of a string to the cup and the other end to a large button. Swing the string slowly, trying to catch it in the cup.

BOWLING

Save empty detergent bottles. Set up the bottles on the floor like bowling pins. Roll a ball on the floor to knock down the bottles.

COLOR MATCH

You'll need an egg carton. Color each egg carton compartment a different color. Collect old buttons and have the children match the color with the egg carton compartment color.

ALPHABET MATCH GAME

Using 26 tops from gallon-size plastic milk bottles, print one alphabet letter on each bottle top with a marker. Cut the lids off three egg cartons. Print one alphabet letter in the bottom of each compartment in the egg cartons. Match the alphabet tops with the letters in the egg cartons.

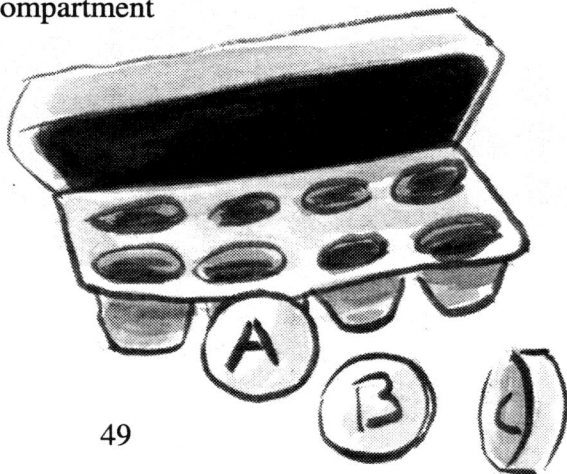

RED LIGHT-GREEN LIGHT

Cut large circles from green and red construction paper. Print "Go" on the green circle and "Stop" on the red circle. Glue popsicle sticks to the bottom of each circle to make signs. Hold up the green sign, and the children walk forward. When the red sign is held up, the children must stop. The first child to reach the adult becomes the new traffic director.

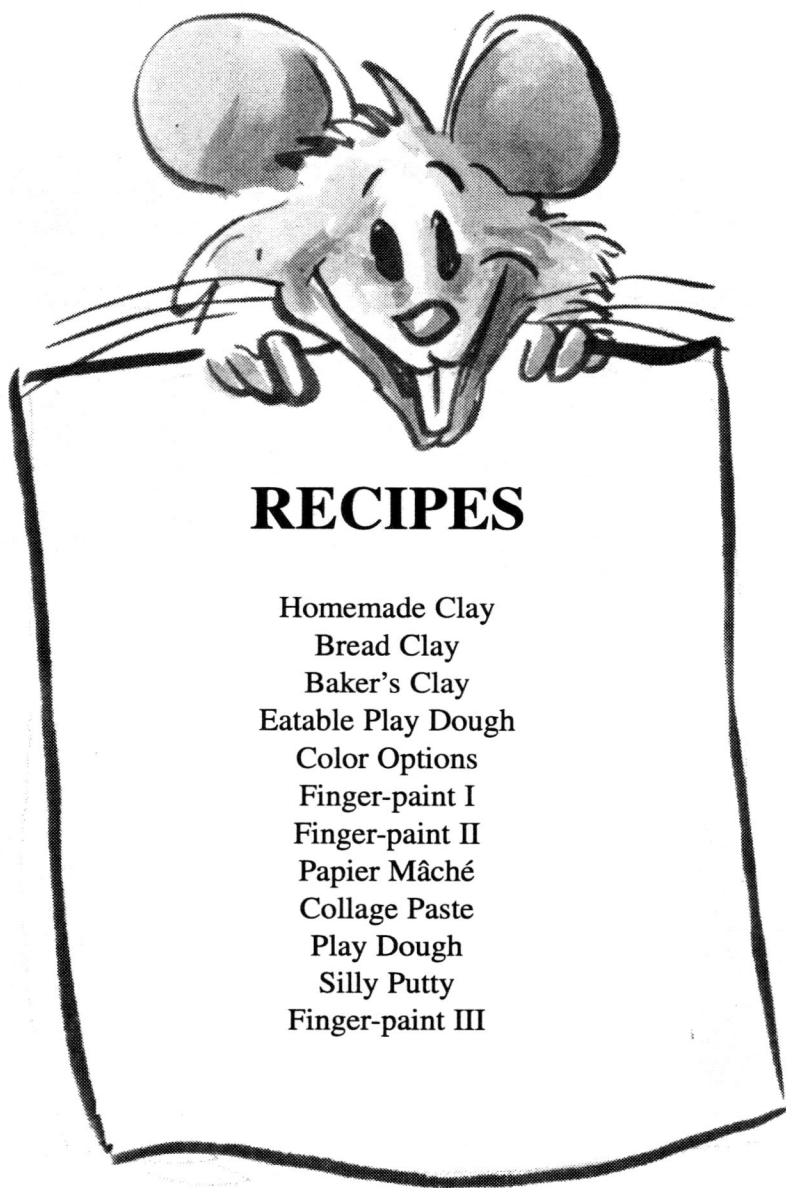

RECIPES

HOMEMADE CLAY

2 cups flour
1/2 cup salt
1/2 cup water
1 tbsp. vegetable oil
Food coloring, optional

Mix the ingredients well and knead to form a smooth consistency. This mixture can be used in most ways clay is used. Store in an airtight container between uses.

Making this clay is almost as much fun as using it. Let the child help. If small bits are consumed, it won't hurt the child. For very young or for children who routinely put clay in their mouths, see the edible clay in this kit.

BREAD CLAY

2 cups fine bread crumbs
4 tbsp. white glue
2 tsp. vinegar or lemon juice
Powdered tempera, optional

Fresh bread crumbs work best, and these can be made by whirling some small pieces of bread in a blender for a few seconds. Add powdered tempera to produce a brilliant color dough. This clay can be molded and then left to dry.

BAKER'S CLAY

4 cups flour
1 cup salt
1 1/2 cup water
Food coloring, optional

Mix the ingredients and knead well. If the dough is too sticky, add a little more flour. After your child has made his or her desired object, place on a foil-covered cookie sheet for baking. Bake at 250 degrees F. until firm — usually about 2 hours.

EATABLE PLAY DOUGH

1 tbsp. honey
1 cup instant dry milk
1 cup peanut butter

Mix ingredients together and knead until smooth.

This is a wonderful "first" clay for young children because it's made from good food, so it can't hurt them to nibble. Older children can have fun creating monsters and then eating them.

COLOR OPTIONS

There are times when a project is started only to discover that there is no food coloring in the house to complete it. That doesn't have to be the end of the play or mean a trip to the market. There are coloring agents in the house right now that can be used in place of commercial food colorings. As long as food items are used, there is no danger to the child. Use your imagination.

Mustard — yellow
Powdered fruit drinks
Kool-Aid
Soy Sauce or Worcestershire Sauce — brown
Powdered Gatorade
French Dressing

FINGER-PAINT I

3 tbsp. cornstarch
3 tbsp. cold water
2 cups boiling water

Mix the starch and cold water until creamy. Add the boiling water and mix well. This provides the medium for the paint. Add food colors or powdered tempera paints to color your finger-paints and let your children have fun.

No one need ever be without resources to entertain children!

FINGER-PAINT II

3 tbsp. flour
3 tbsp. water

Mix flour and water together, add food coloring or pow-dered tempera paint.

This second recipe is very much like the first but makes a smaller amount. Flour is used as the alternate because almost everyone has it in the home.

PAPIER MÂCHÉ

Mix flour and water until it is a gravy-like consisten-cy. Adjust the amounts of each ingredient according to the size of the project planned.

Newspaper is the easiest, most readily available paper to use with paste. Tear or cut strips of news-paper about an inch wide and set aside. A few strips at a time, soak the paper in the paste and wipe off excess as they are lifted out. Drape over mold and allow to dry. Inflated balloons, branches, bent wire and strings tied to a frame make nice molds over which the papier mâché strips can be laid. Large plastic dolls can have their "broken" legs and arms fixed with papier mâché casts.

COLLAGE PASTE

3 tsp. flour
2 tsp. water

Mix flour and water until smooth.

Use with magazine cutout pictures, scraps of cloth, leaves and twigs, sand or small gravel, glitter — any light material that can be glued to a sheet of paper or cardboard. The textures and layers achieved are as important to the child as the colors.

PLAY DOUGH

1 cup flour
1 tbsp. vegetable oil
1 cup water
1/2 cup salt
Food coloring, optional

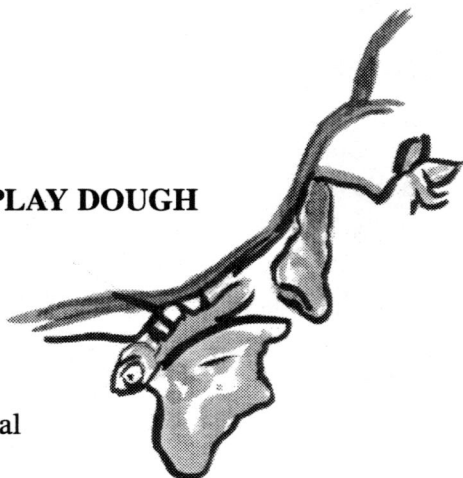

Cook over medium heat until mixture thickens. Then knead. Play dough should be stored in an airtight container.

The cooking part is yours, but the fun from this dough can be shared by both you and your child.

SILLY PUTTY

1 part liquid starch
1 part Elmer's school glue

Pour the glue into the starch and work it carefully with the hands until it becomes smooth and stretchy. This takes about 15 minutes. As the starch is absorbed, the stickiness leaves. Now the children can take over and do the final kneading and stretching. Store in airtight container.

The real fun of this mixture is that it can be pulled out very thin and reshaped, just like commercial silly putty. It lasts several days before becoming unusable.

FINGER-PAINT III

1/2 cup flour
1/2 cup salt
water for consistency
food coloring as desired

Blend well and store in jars.

A nice thick paint can be made for young children who really like to get their hands into their projects.

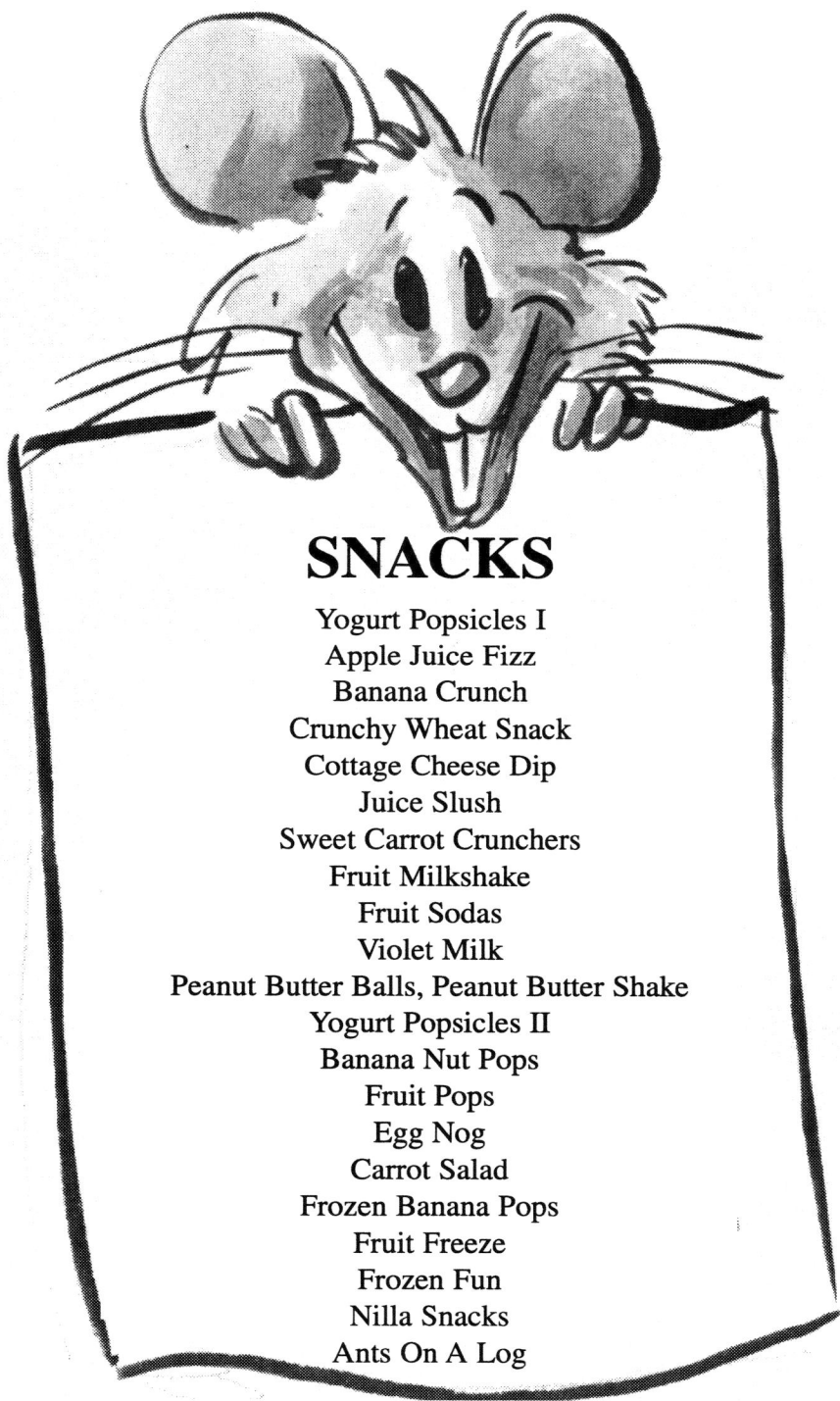

SNACKS

Yogurt Popsicles I
Apple Juice Fizz
Banana Crunch
Crunchy Wheat Snack
Cottage Cheese Dip
Juice Slush
Sweet Carrot Crunchers
Fruit Milkshake
Fruit Sodas
Violet Milk
Peanut Butter Balls, Peanut Butter Shake
Yogurt Popsicles II
Banana Nut Pops
Fruit Pops
Egg Nog
Carrot Salad
Frozen Banana Pops
Fruit Freeze
Frozen Fun
Nilla Snacks
Ants On A Log

YOGURT POPSICLES I

2 cups yogurt
6 oz. frozen orange juice
honey to taste (teaspoon usually)
2 tsp. vanilla

Mix well and freeze in molds or paper cups. Insert popsicle sticks when partially frozen.

Here is a treat for those hot summer afternoons that provides great taste and good nutrition at the same time. An excellent substitute for sugary and artificially flavored treats ... and just as much fun!

APPLE JUICE FIZZ

12 oz. can apple juice concentrate
32 oz. bottle carbonated soda (club soda)
24 oz. water

Stir above ingredients together in pitcher.
Options: any kind of fruit juice (or combinations of juices) can be used.

This is a good way to extend a bottle of soda and add a little nutrition at the same time. Children love it even though they are drinking some healthy juices.

BANANA CRUNCH

banana, peeled and sliced into coins
1/2 cup honey
1/4 cup granola or wheat germ

Put the honey in one bowl, the granola or wheat germ in
another. Demonstrate how to pick up a slice of banana
with a toothpick and dip it into the honey, then the granola
or wheat germ in turn. This makes a healthy snack.

Because this snack takes a little dexterity in keeping the
banana slice on the toothpick, it can slow down and extend
the time of eating. By the time a child has picked up,
dipped and then eaten a banana in this way, the urge to eat
is often satisfied and the child is ready to go about his/her
play. It's also a lot of fun.

CRUNCHY WHEAT SNACK

4 cups bite-size shredded wheat
1/3 cup melted margarine
1 1/2 cups stick pretzels
   (broken in half)
1/2 cup dry roasted peanuts
1/2 cup raisins
garlic powder

Spread the shredded wheat in
the bottom of an oblong cake pan. Cover with melted margarine and sprinkle with some garlic powder. Bake at 350
degrees for 15 minutes. Add the pretzel sticks, peanuts,
and raisins. Store in an airtight container.

COTTAGE CHEESE DIP

1/3 cup milk
1 pint cottage cheese
1/2 pkg. onion or vegetable dry soup mix
1 can tuna fish, drained

Blend together by hand or in a blender. Refrigerate 1 hour. Serve this dip with raw vegetables — carrot and celery sticks, sliced zucchini or florets of broccoli and cauliflower.

If skim milk and low-fat cottage cheese are used, this makes a very low calorie dip which is every bit as tasty as dips with a sour cream base! Parents will enjoy it as much as the children.

JUICE SLUSH

1/3 cup nonfat dry milk
6 oz. frozen juice (orange, apple, grape, fruit)
1 cup water
1/2 cup crushed ice

Blend together quickly.

Hot summer afternoons never had it so good! Here is a low-calorie treat your child will love, yet provides good nutrition and wonderful flavor. Vary the frozen juice for some creative taste treats.

SWEET CARROT CRUNCHERS

2 cups sliced carrots (sticks)
pineapple juice to cover

Soak the carrot sticks in the pineapple juice for 2 to 3 hours in the refrigerator.

The carrots pick up just enough sweetness from the pineapple to be particularly delicious and the crisping in the refrigerator makes them extra tempting. Put these out as "finger foods" and watch them disappear!

FRUIT MILKSHAKE

1 cup milk
1 cup fruit (banana, peach, strawberries, blueberries, and
    so forth)

Blend milk and fruit in blender.

Do you have a child who doesn't drink enough milk? No more! Mix up this healthy shake and be ready to wipe away those milky mustaches. Kids really love this frothy treat.

FRUIT SODAS

equal amounts of club soda and fruit juice
crushed ice, optional

Mix the same amount of club soda and fruit juice to create a healthier drink for kids. Blended with crushed ice, this tasty beverage instantly becomes a fruity slush for hot summer afternoons.

More nutritious than straight pop or syrupy slushy treats, this recipe is just as much fun for the children and less expensive for parents.

VIOLET MILK

1/4 cup grape juice
1 cup milk
1 banana, sliced

Mix the ingredients in a blender. The milk turns a lovely violet color and has the rich taste of grapes and bananas. A wonderfully healthy treat for children that's just odd enough to attract their attention, too.

Use skim milk for a really low-calorie drink or special treat.

PEANUT BUTTER BALLS

1/2 cup raisins
1/4 cup apple juice concentrate
1/4 cup peanut butter
1/4 cup-low fat dry milk
1 tsp. vanilla
1 tsp. cinnamon
1 cup grape nuts

Heat raisins and apple juice concentrate in a sauce pan. Boil about 2 minutes. Pour raisins and apple juice concentrate in a blender and mix. Blend in remainder of ingredients. Shape the mixture into small balls.

Refrigerate 1 hour.

PEANUT BUTTER SHAKE

1 ripe banana
1 cup milk
1 tbsp. creamy peanut butter

Blend together in the blender for a nice thick shake. Serve with a straw and watch the children smile.

A wonderfully healthy treat for children with all the flavors they love. Great as a party beverage!

YOGURT POPSICLES II

1 cup plain yogurt
1 cup fruit juice, any flavor
1 banana, sliced
1 tsp. vanilla
1 tsp. honey

Blend ingredients together and pour into small paper cups. Place popsicle sticks in each cup when mixture is partially frozen. Allow several hours to freeze this treat.

This is an extra special summer afternoon treat. It's all good food, too! Give it to your children with a clear conscience. So tasty the children won't care that it's good for them.

BANANA NUT POPS

Banana, cut across the middle
Syrup (any kind the children
   like)
Finely chopped nuts

Carefully insert a popsicle stick into half a banana. Dip or roll in syrup, then roll in the chopped nuts. This snack can be eaten just as it is made, or frozen for a cooling, crunchy treat.

Try a variety of syrups and different nuts, chopped in the food processor or blender. Cake decorations make this treat particularly festive for parties and special occasions.

FRUIT POPS

Freeze fruit juice in ice trays or small paper cups. Use toothpicks or popsicle sticks for handles.

An old standby for healthy frozen treats. Vary this by mixing juices or freezing in different small containers — ice cube squares, little cups, cupcake cups, free-form aluminum foil containers pressed around small toys. Use your imagination.

EGG NOG

1 egg
1 cup milk
1/2 banana
2 drops vanilla
Dash of cinnamon

Blend together in blender.

Practically all the protein and calcium needed for a meal is here in this great drink. Give your child a straw and let him/her enjoy it.

CARROT SALAD

1. Wash and grate 2 carrots.
2. Add 1/2 cup raisins (optional).
3. Stir in 1 tsp. lemon juice.
4. Mix in 2 tbsp. plain yogurt.

Variations: mayonnaise or sour cream may be substituted for plain yogurt.

FROZEN BANANA POPS

1. Peel banana carefully.
2. Cut the banana in half.
3. Poke an ice cream stick into each banana half.
4. Put each banana pop on a small piece of aluminum foil. Gently wrap the foil tightly around the pop.
5. Put the banana pops into the freezer for about 5 or 6 hours.

Options: The frozen pops can be eaten plain, or coated with honey, chocolate, or syrup. Pour honey, chocolate, or syrup onto a small plate and roll the frozen pop around until it is coated.

FRUIT FREEZE

1. Peel a banana and put it in a mixing bowl. Mash with a fork.
2. Add 1/2 cup crushed pineapple along with some juice.
3. Add 3/4 cup orange juice. Stir.
4. Distribute the mixture in muffin cups set into a muffin pan.
5. Place aluminum foil over muffin pans and place in freezer for 7 to 8 hours.
6. Press the bottom of the muffin cup to make the frozen fruit pop out.

FROZEN FUN

Using any of your store-bought products that come in small plastic containers, such as apple sauce, yogurt, pudding snacks, remove the cover and insert a popsicle stick. Put in freezer. When frozen, run warm water over the bottom of the container to make removal easier. Your child now has a nutritious frozen snack.

NILLA SNACKS

Nilla Wafers can be used in a variety of ways. Dip them in ice cream or pudding for a creamy treat. Or make tiny sandwiches with them using frosting, fruit, peanut butter or jelly as fillings.

ANTS ON A LOG

celery sticks
peanut butter or cheese whiz
raisins

Clean celery sticks well and cut into 3- to 5-inch lengths. Fill the inside with peanut butter or cheese whiz and sprinkle with raisins.

Serve this nutritious food as a snack or with a meal to spark a child's interest. This snack can brighten a rainy day simply because of its funny name.

SUGGESTED ACTIVITIES

1. Make a list from kindergarten through senior year of what you want to be when you grow up.
2. Decorate tricycles and bicycles for a parade in your neighborhood.
3. Plan a campfire and roast hot dogs.
4. Visit the zoo.
5. Visit a museum.
6. Visit a historical site.
7. Shovel a neighbor's driveway.
8. Keep a list of all the books you read.
9. Tell a story from memory.
10. Learn a new poem.
11. Learn a new history story each week. Send gifts to refugees.
12. Make holiday gifts for the needy.
13. Visit a dairy, horse, chicken, turkey, or beef farm.
14. Have a picnic in the woods.
15. Have a librarian tell you about the books in your library you should read.
16. Collect picture postcards.
17. Go on a hayride.
18. Go for a boat ride.
19. Go to your local library; most libraries have story time for children.
20. Make homemade ice cream.
21. Go swimming.
22. Make a butterfly collection.
23. Collect napkins from restaurants.
24. Plant a small garden.
25. Start a stamp collection.
26. Go on a bird search.

27. Go camping.
28. Exchange books, toys, and games with classmates.
29. Make a picture collection of animals.
30. Plan a surprise party for your parents.
31. Organize a singing group.
32. Collect used clothes for the needy.
33. Go on a train ride.
34. Plant a flower bed.
35. Make soap earrings.
36. Use old dishsoap containers, with colored water for snow-painting.
37. Put on a hobby show in your neighborhood.
38. Read a children's story.
39. Read the newspaper.
40. Go ice skating.
41. Go bowling.
42. Go roller skating.
43. Organize a basketball game.
44. Make a birdfeeder from a kit.
45. Go to a floral store, nursery, or a greenhouse.
46. Take a tour of your local church.
47. Visit grandma and grandpa.
48. Invite friends or relatives for lunch.
49. Visit a local police station.
50. Visit a local fire station.
51. Let a teacher or a doctor give children an opportunity to ask questions about their work.
52. Take a walk in the country.
53. Have a picnic in the park.
54. Go rock hunting.
55. Make a leaf collection.
56. Make a birdhouse from a kit.
57. Organize a story hour for after school.

57. Organize a story hour for after school.
58. Go hiking.
59. Save money for a special project.
60. Go kite flying.
61. Remember to say please and thank you.
62. Show home movies.
63. Ask grandma if she has home movies of mom or dad.
64. Write letters to distant friends or relatives.
65. Read a good book.
66. Catch fireflies.
67. Catch butterflies.
68. Catch caterpillars in the fall of the year; watch them make cocoons.

INDEX